# BE A HARD TARGET
## IN A TARGET RICH ENVIRONMENT

# BE A HARD TARGET
# IN A TARGET RICH ENVIRONMENT

Z. F. LEMON

**PALMETTO**
**P U B L I S H I N G**
Charleston, SC
www.PalmettoPublishing.com

© 2024 Z. F. Lemon

All rights reserved.

No portion of this book may be reproduced, stored in a retrieval system, or transmitted in any form by any means–electronic, mechanical, photocopy, recording, or other–except for brief quotations in printed reviews, without prior permission of the author.

Paperback ISBN: 979-8-8229-5404-5

*"We cannot continue to rely only on our military in order to achieve the national security objectives that we've set. We've got to have a civilian national security force that's just as powerful, just as strong, just as well funded."*
-Barack Obama

Now, let us make this statement applicable on a personal level…

You and I cannot continue to rely solely on the police in order to achieve the personal security hoped for. We have to be just as capable, equipped, and prepared as our local law enforcement.

I will be making a concerted effort to make you a **Hard Target in a Target Rich Environment.**

**You** are your own first responder until first responders arrive.

By no means am I suggesting that you take anything other than your very own protection (or your loved ones) into your own hands. I do not subscribe that anyone acts as a vigilante.

# CONTENTS

Topic 1. The Things That Shaped Me ................................. 1

Topic 2. Avoidance ................................................................ 7

Topic 3. OODA & The Cooper Color Code ..................... 13

Topic 4. Tools of the Trade ................................................ 23

Topic 5. The Clock Method ............................................... 35

Topic 6. Preparation ........................................................... 43

Topic 7. Final Thoughts and Good Advice ....................... 49

# TOPIC 1
## THE THINGS THAT SHAPED ME

This is probably the most difficult part about writing this book. I am a retired US Marine with 3 combat deployments. I am currently diagnosed with at least two mental disorders to include PTSD. I am a consistent gym rat that always carries protection and my GSD (German Shepherd Dog) is always by my side. I'm 6'1" and a solid 250 pounds and I still don't always feel safe.

When I was 5-6 years old, I had a female babysitter that forced me to perform sexual acts on her. I was afraid to tell my mom about it because the sitter threatened me. I had another sitter that worked in the public school system that constantly referred to me as "Sissy." I have no idea why she did that, but it still bothers me. I discovered decades later that she was the victim of domestic abuse from her husband. Hurt people, hurt people. In elementary school, there were kids there that looked like they should have been in High school. This was before "No Child Left Behind."

If you failed the 2nd grade three times consecutively, oh well, you were bigger, stronger, faster, and angrier than the other 2nd graders. I was one of those 2nd graders. Not the big angry ones, one of the little ones in the appropriate grade. On top of being held back multiple times, I strongly believe that those kids started school late as well. I told my mom that some of my classmates were taller than her, but she thought that I was exaggerating. I'm not sure that I was. My mom was 5'9." My mom and dad were divorced before I turned 6, so my hero was the Incredible Hulk. He was strong. He was never victimized. He was never small. While in middle school there was a high school kid that made disgusting threats while we were on the school bus. I am certain that he was serious. He possessed the intent, and capability, I just never gave him the opportunity.

While in middle school, I never weighed over 110 pounds. No need to feel sorry for me, these are simply the facts. After I graduated high school, I joined the Airforce. I wasn't tough enough to join the Marines yet.

The Air Force wasn't too bad. After we finished security police school, we went to Air Base Ground Defense School. This school was in Ft. Dix, New Jersey and was taught by the Army. A month after my four year enlistment concluded, I joined the Marines. I did a little over 16 years in the Corps. I was primarily a Combat Engineer. Combat Engineers did IED defeat. Improvised Explosive Devices were everywhere during my 2nd and 3rd combat deployments. They were not so prevalent during OIF 1. I was also a Marine Corps Martial Arts instructor (Black belt). My prior service in the Air Force, as well as the time at Ft. Dix really prepared me for the Corps. I graduated platoon honor grad. The Corps was exactly what I needed. We learned a martial art back then called: L.I.N.E training. L.I.N.E stands for: Linear, Involuntary, Neural-override, Engagement. This fighting technique was for the battlefield, not for a typical barroom brawl. L.I.N.E ended with a finishing technique that had the Marine executing a leg sweep and then driving the cutting edge of his or her boot down through the enemy's eye socket. Effectively ending the fight. In a self-defense scenario, I would advise executing the leg sweep and then stomping the ankle. This should prevent him from chasing you down. We will dive into additional effective tactics throughout the book.

# TOPIC 2
## AVOIDANCE

# THE BEST FIGHT IS THE ONE YOU AVOID

Let us talk about avoidance. The best situation to overcome is the one you avoid in the first place. Did you hear about the Spanish couple in India? The married couple were on a motorbike trip in India. They were unable to find lodging at a hotel so they pitched a tent. The report states that seven men gang raped the female tourist and hit the husband repeatedly. As I write this, only 3 of the men have been caught. An average of nearly 90 rapes a day were reported in India in 2022, according to data from the National Crime Records Bureau. When traveling to a foreign country, look up the country in the World Factbook. Determine if the country is rampant with crime. Look specifically at violent crimes. Also, if you are backpacking and camping, what type of improvised weapon are you allowed to have with you. Would a machete or camp ax be ok? You are your initial first responder until help can arrive. Be aware of the local crime rate and know what you may have as a weapon for protection. Don't just have the weapon, have a visual of how to use it. Go through various scenarios in your head. If you are fortunate enough to have a wife that is all about situational awareness too, she should have a weapon that she is familiar with and knows how to use. Could the couple have brought a dog along? A dog can be a great deterrent. I read or heard decades ago, "don't go to stupid places with stupid people and do stupid things." This phrase to live by will reduce the chances of you experiencing a violent encounter by 70%. If you find yourself out in public or on public transportation and you lock eyes with a want to be tough guy, and he says, "you got a problem?" Just swallow your pride and let him know that you are just coming off a double shift and that you must have zoned out for a second. With avoidance, it is often about swallowing your pride. You don't need the hassle of a pointless fight. You could get hurt or hurt someone. If you end up in court, anything could happen. Another avoidance technique is to wear sunglasses when feasible. This prevents locking eyes with any potential trouble makers. If you are vulnerable - this could be elderly, a small woman or man, disabled person, or transgender, a minority; predators often prey on the vulnerable.

The youth are also susceptible to being victimized. A few days ago some pre-teen girls were having a sleepover. The newly divorced father of the hostess drugged the girls. When one of the girls started to feel the effects of the sedative, she texted her mom. She told her mom to make up a story about there being a family emergency. This was quick thinking and kept a bad situation from becoming even worse. Ultimately, the girls were all removed from the home. There is currently a missing 32 year old male from an American town. He was planning to walk to the local store and was never seen nor heard from again. He is relatively young, 5'10" and 200 pounds. How can he just be gone? The dangers are all around us. Look at your local news. Determine the method of operation these predators are using. Study the Cooper Color Code, live in the yellow. Go over scenarios in your head so that you are never in the Black. I'm wondering what time of day / night the young man left for the store. Was his cell phone fully charged? Does he have family and friends that can freely track his whereabouts? What about the pre-teen sleepover? The only adult was a newly divorced middle aged man? Hmmm, I do not have a daughter but if I did, she would not have been allowed to attend. 90% of divorced guys are not creeps. I just cannot ignore the 10% that are. Maybe it's only 5% that are creeps, or even fewer - I just don't like it.

# TOPIC 3
## OODA & THE COOPER COLOR CODE

# THE **COOPER COLOR CODE** CONSISTS OF FIVE COLORS

## WHITE

Your guard is down, you feel safe and secure. You are not anticipating any trouble. You are often like this when you are at home with the doors and windows locked and the alarm is set.

## YELLOW

There is a heightened state of alertness. You've noticed something that could be a potential threat. You are not sure but you will continue to monitor the situation.

## ORANGE

There is a guy wearing all black and a trench coat despite 85 degree weather. You are getting a bad vibe. You are aware of all of the nearest exits. You are coming up with a plan of action.

## RED

Now it's on! A weapon has been revealed and it is fight or flight for you.

## BLACK

Black is the final color. We use this color in the U.S. Marine Corps. Black is being combat ineffective. Freezing. Unresponsive despite the chaos unfolding in your presence. An unfortunate example of being in the "Black" is when you see a member of the Uvalde entry team stop and apply hand sanitizer. Despite the carnage happening in the school, he is applying a hand cleanser? The Cooper Color Code is all about the combat mindset. You do not need to be in a warzone to make it applicable.

The OODA Loop is a military derived thinking concept. The OODA loop is a decision-making model developed by military strategist and United States Air Force Colonel John Boyd. He applied the concept to the operational level during military campaigns. It is often applied to understand commercial operations and learning processes as well. Observe, Orient, Decide.

How can we increase our chances of being safe and secure? How do we reduce our chances of being victimized? Awareness is huge. Know what is going on in your community. Know what's happening in the town next to yours? Reverse engineer potential issues and crimes. What happened to the 32-year-old that walked to his neighborhood store? What would you have done differently? Keep your phone charged and have trusted loved ones that are able to track your movements. Also, rats travel in packs, so when you can, bring a friend along to the store with you. If you are taking a Lyft or Uber, Confirm the plate # before getting in. Every time my wife gets into a Lyft or an Uber, I am alerted as she is on her way and when she arrives safely. I'm usually with her but the feature still works. There have been instances where people have gotten into a vehicle that was not their rideshare. Unfortunately, oftentimes they did not survive. This is avoidable. Try not to travel alone when you can help it. At my airport, there is a designated rideshare area. I saw a vehicle pull up and a man jumped out from behind the wheel. A lone female says, "Jacob right?" The driver answers, "yes." Was he really Jacob? I have no idea. You must confirm your rideshare in a better manner than that. My wife was with me and noticed the young lady's mistake as well.

I recommend that you always keep a knife on you. I once kept a folder on me at all times. It had a thumb loop which made it rapidly deployable. Now I carry a 4" fixed blade. It's an Esse tactical fixed blade with slight serrations. It comes with a hard plastic sheath and can be easily carried in your front or back pocket. Please see the picture below.

Be sure to know the laws of your state, city, and town. Some places have length restrictions. Length is less important if you attack vulnerable places on the body. If your life is truly in danger you have to be willing to attack the eyes and or throat. You are valuable. Your family loves you. Who is this creep to take you away - permanently I should add, no, not today. Fight as if your life depends on it, because it does. It is not commonplace to imagine thrusting your thumbs or an ink pen or a knife through the eye of someone trying to rape or kill you. It is essential that you are prepared mentally should such an encounter ever occur. Develop a warrior mindset so that you can tap into it when required. Do not confuse living cautiously with paranoia. We live in a world where bad things happen to good people on a continuous basis. Be as prepared as possible.

I had my concealed carry permit in multiple states. I felt safer with my 9mm Springfield than I did without it. However, I do not go to stupid places with stupid people and do stupid things. I started running scenarios in my head. If I were to get stopped by law enforcement for a moving violation, could they possibly overreact due to my gun possession? I started feeling like it may be more likely that the cops overreact and I end up dead, than if I had to legitimately defend myself using my firearm. Look up the case with Philando Castille. He was authorized to have his firearm but was killed by a police officer. The cop seemed overwhelmed by the fact that Philando had a gun. Keep in mind, it was not dark out and there was a child in the car. The cop still grossly overreacted and ended Philando's life.

So, I have decided to keep my firearms for home defense. If you get through my locks and German Shepherd dog while setting off the alarm system, I will be ready with a firearm with a high-capacity magazine. As I go out on errands, I try to get everything accomplished during the day. I usually have my dog with me, and I carry a fixed blade pocket knife. This is just my personal decision. I strongly suggest that you work out the pros and cons for each option as it pertains to you and the types of law enforcement officers that you are likely to encounter in your state and community.

Should you ever find yourself in a position where it is necessary to defend yourself, be decisive, intentional, and violent. Violence of action is paramount. With every strike, attempt to go through the assailant. If you strike the nose, attempt to get to the back of his head via the nose. This is an intense mentality, and it may be a new concept for most good guys that do not wish to be a victim, however, human predators effectively use violence as a tool. They strike with the intention of intimidation, fear, forced compliance, severe injury, and death. They want to do this while you remain within the scope of "societal norms." They do not want you to go from yellow to red. They do not want you to drive your car key through their orbital orpheus. I'm here to tell you that you must be prepared to do just that. Don't think that you can just cause the predator "pain" and he'll leave you alone. Predators are often desperate and determined. Pain will not stop them. Damage will. There is a difference. There is a saying - pain don't hurt. Do not let up until the predator is no longer able to pose a threat. This means that he is unconscious, (Blunt force trauma to the head) combat ineffective (his eye is gouged and there is NO fight left in him) or he is dead. It is NOT over until his status is described above. It is NOT over until you can safely call the cops. The cops will be the 2nd responders. You had to be your very own 1st responder.

Predators hunt for victims. Do everything in your power to make them select someone other than you. Walk confidently, projecting an image of self-awareness as well as situational awareness. This means that you are not looking down at your phone. You are not distracted; however, you appear aware and alert. If you are alone and just got out of your vehicle, grasp your keys in such a way that makes them readily available for defense via offense. This can be done by protruding them beyond your knuckles (laced between fingers) or by allowing one to extend out of a hammered grip fist as if you were holding an ice pick.

This can act as a visual deterrent. Be prepared to use any improvised weapon initially to defend yourself, all the while strategizing how you would transition to your primary weapon if necessary. When I go to the grocery store, I keep all of the bags in the push cart / buggy. This way I am able to keep both arms free for defense. If you are holding a sack of groceries, mentally practice dropping the bag should the need present itself. You just bought these items with hard earned money and some of the items purchased are fragile. Letting them crash to the pavement is not second nature. You have to consciously tell yourself that you will drop them without a second thought in order to defend yourself and loved one's.

Be familiar with the term **Pre-incident indicator.** An overt example of this would be a shady character leaning on the hood of your car in the grocery store parking lot as you exit the store. Should this happen, stop in your tracks and act as if you've just received a call on your cell. Be animated and act as if the person that you are on the phone with is parked in the lot as well. Point at a car and then give a thumbs up sign as if the two of you see each other. Next go back into the store as if you have to pick up one more item. Look at your wrist as if you are pressed for time. Hopefully this will get the trouble maker to move along. He should be under the impression that you are not alone and you will be right back out. Do not approach the car until the suspicious subject is gone. You can also make an actual call to someone that you can count on to let them know what is going on. While moving through parking lots such as big box stores and or Wal-mart, be watchful of a technique called bracketing. Predators use this to place you at a great disadvantage. One guy will be posted up behind you while another crafty villain will be in front of you. Before you know it, you are in between two scumbags that have bad intentions. Be alert for pre-incident indicators in every large parking lot. Always feel free to go back into the store if things just do not seem right. When possible go to stores that provide security officers. Feel free to ask them for a courtesy escort to your vehicle when feasible.

# TOPIC 4
## TOOLS OF THE TRADE

# LET US SPEAK ABOUT SOME TOOLS OF THE TRADE

Studies show that most home invasions happen between 6:00 P.M. and 6:00 A.M. Anyone bold and desperate enough to enter your home uninvited should be taken as a serious threat. My tools start on my fence with a beware of the dog sign on my gate. Please see below. I also have a no soliciting sign at my front door. I have cameras on my home and an 83 lb male German Shepherd that barks loudly every time anyone comes to the door. A lady came to my door yesterday at around 2:00 P.M. in the afternoon. She said that she was conducting a survey. I asked through the door, "how can I help?" She was not able to articulate her business in a satisfactory manner. Now, I have a few tattoos, but she had a lot more than me, as hers went up both sides of her neck and to her face. I could not confirm her affiliation from the tattoos I observed but I just did not feel comfortable opening the door. There are plenty of home footage recordings showing a homeowner opening the door for a woman and then a couple guys appear out of nowhere and rush to and through the front door. I have a 4.5 inch fixed blade knife hanging on the end of the hat rack near the front door. Plus I keep my Esee 4" knife in my front pocket at all times. It is your home, be prepared to defend it. I highly suggest that you get a dog and a firearm for home defense. Your dog should ideally be a "man stopper." If you are restricted and can only have a little toy breed, get one that barks at strange noises. This is a tool - it is an early warning device. If you have the pick of the litter as you choose a new puppy, walk away from the pups and drop something on the ground. Take note of the pup(s) that run toward the sound. This is a great indicator that the dog will be an awesome watchdog. This will serve as a highly valuable tool. Your secondary early warning device will be your home alarm system. So, beware of dog signs, a dog, an alarm system, cameras, and a firearm and or blade. Remember, keep outside lights on and inside lights off while you are asleep. Another tool is a flashlight. I have several. Some of my lights are mounted to my firearms, others are handheld and are equipped with DNA catchers. See photo below.

These are all tools used to maximize your ability to survive. Using these tools in unison make you a hard target. These tools are great when stacked up against a potential predator, however, when I decided not to open my door for the tattooed lady "conducting a survey," I was using the greatest tool of all, the one between my ears.

We all need backup tools as well. For instance, if it is warm out and I am wearing shorts, I may carry my 3" Esee fixed blade knife. I also have a cold steel recon 1 folder. Some apparel make it so that you have to make adjustments. See photo below.

If I am in my pajamas late at night and I need to let the dog out, I still take the time to arm myself with a knife before I release him into the backyard. Below are pocket lights and pocketknife examples.

Rapid deployment is an absolute necessity. This is aided by knives with thumb loops or thumb studs. Assisted opening knives are great too. Just be sure to check your local and state laws.

With a blade, it is important to know how you want to hold it for defensive purposes. There is the saber grip. This is when your four fingers are wrapped around the handle and your thumb is resting on top, behind the blade. The knuckles of your fingers facing the ground while the thumb knuckle is facing upwards. The blade should be pointing towards your threat. With the saber grip the blade is simply an extension of your fist. It is convenient to assume a boxing stance and use the blade just as a jab (thrust) hook, and uppercut. The blade can be in your rear hand or forward (jab) hand. I practice both options. I imagine that if I am in front of one assailant, I'd have the knife in my rear hand. I'd set up my thrusts and slashes with my lead hand jab. If there is more than one goon (bad guy), I'd have my weapon in my forward hand. This would be my right foot and right hand forward. This is called the southpaw stance. If you have your left hand and left foot forward - you are in the orthodox stance.

Another great option is the ice pick grip (or reverse grip). Hold the blade just as you would an ice pick. The blade should be pointing downward with the sharp edge facing your adversary. Now to use this grip, use hammer fist strikes. Vertical (downward), Horizontal and Diagonal strikes should be your effort here. Keep your motions tight, never extending much past your body's center line. Imagine that you are holding a hammer but do not strike in a predictable manner. A predictable hammer strike may be easily blocked or avoided. Incorporate your elbow and wrist in order to make your offense unorthodox.

The Hammer grip is another option. With this grip - you hold the blade just like a hammer, sharp edge towards the adversary, blade pointing up. Use thrusts and slashes while maintaining a hammer grip. See examples of the grips on the following pages.

**SABER GRIP**

BE A HARD TARGET

**ICE-PICK GRIP**

**HAMMER GRIP**

You also have to consider how you desire to carry a knife. Appendix carry is centered on the front of your body above your crotch. You have scout carry, when you carry the blade horizontally on the small of your back. Or, pocket carry, this can be accomplished with a pocketknife or a fixed blade. Practice your draw and determine the carry that suits you best. Take note of the photos below.

You need to be able to draw your blade and assume the grip you wish to use all in one motion. Practice, practice, practice. However, be careful and be safe. This goes double if you elect to carry a firearm. For some knives, there are plastic training versions. This is a great training aid and a wise investment. There are rubber training pistols available as well. Never train with a loaded pistol. And by rule, ALL pistols are ALWAYS loaded. With that said, never train with a real pistol unless you are on the range and it is marksmanship training. If you carry a pistol, make sure that you have a concealed carry permit. If you live in a city that borders another state, get a permit for that state as well if there is no reciprocity agreement. For blades, make sure that as you cross into different cities and states, that you are still in compliance with the laws of the newly entered town. How bad would it be to get locked up on a weapon infraction. Now you're being housed with hundreds of thugs that are mostly armed with shanks (improvised knives). Such a scenario must be avoided at all costs.

# TOPIC 5
## THE CLOCK METHOD

# TACTICS & DEFENSE

Here is a concept that I would like for you to try. This will help to make you a **Hard Target in a Target Rich Environment.** Imagine a circular wall clock, but it is huge - it is the size of a large living room and lying flat on the ground. The clock has numbers 1-12 (1 through 12) and you are in the center. The direction that you are facing is 12 O'clock. If someone is approaching you head on, they are at your 12 O'clock. If someone is to your right, they are at your 3 O'clock. Imagine that you are in the center of the clock facing 12. A potential threat can come at any "time" / number on the clock. You are in the parking lot and approaching you with nefarious intentions is a hoodlum that thinks you are an easy mark (victim). Your color code goes from yellow to red. You must be prepared to deliver a webbed palm strike to his throat. This is when you join all four fingers while your thumb is making your hand form a letter V or L. The palm of your hand is facing the ground. You strike with the web of your hand, the area between the pointing finger and thumb. His trachea is your target. You can execute this strike with your lead hand or rear hand. Shoot the strike out and then rapidly retract your hand. Follow up by kicking his knee. Ideally, you would like to hyper-extend his knee. Use more of a push-kick than a soccer kick. It is like a stomping motion while your foot is elevated high enough to push his knee with the bottom of your foot. This combination, web palm strike to the throat, followed up with an elevated stomp to the knee should afford you the opportunity to escape and call law enforcement. You can train this combo and get very confident in its delivery. This is a devastating combination and may cause permanent damage or death. Make certain that you are justified before use.

This time a crook approaches you from 3 O'clock in between cars in a parking lot. Lift your right foot up and thrust a sidekick right into his knee. Do this with the intention of hyperextending his knee. Now step forward with your rear leg (left leg) and turn to your right using the balls of your feet. This allows you to face the predator. With your weight on your rear (left) leg, lift your forward leg and deliver a kick to the groin. He should be doubled over (bending at the waist). With a hand on each of his forward leaning shoulders, shove him backward onto his butt. Next, stomp his ankle so that he is unable to pursue you as you get away to report the incident. Train this technique on the left side (9 O'clock) as well. The tactic works the same way on the opposite side. Keep in mind, this level of combative defense can cause your assailant serious bodily harm or death. Be certain that you are justified. As soon as there is no longer a threat, stop being the aggressor.

If a mugger approached you from the 5 O'clock position and got you into a headlock, swim over him with your right arm as if you are swimming in a pool performing a breast stroke. Your hand should stop at the mugger's chin. Pull him up right by his chin, forcing his head back and exposing his throat. Now with a hammer fist, strike down on his throat and push him to the ground. This same exact principle works if you are attacked from your 7 O'clock. All you do is swim over with your right arm, cup his chin and pull it up so that it exposes his throat. Now, strike his trachea with your left hammer fist.

If they were to grab hold of you, but not in a headlock from your 5 or 7 O'clock, flip / throw them over the leg that the mugger is nearest. If you can gain the leverage, a hip toss would be ideal. After you flip him, stomp his ankle or knee and flee. Always call the police post incident, do it quickly. The first story received by law enforcement is usually the one they accept. Also, in self-defense, always use the appropriate amount of force to stop the threat. This should be the minimum required to accomplish the desired result. The desired result is getting the bad guy to stop being harmful to you. As soon as he is no longer a threat, you are no longer using combatives.

A thug grabs you from behind, this would be your 6 O'clock. If you can, retrieve your weapon, do so and inflict damage according to the available targets of the mugger. If you have a blade, jam it into the side of his leg with an intentional thrust. Retain a positive grip on the knife. Twist the knife while it is inserted and then pull it out while maintaining positive control of your weapon. If the thug has not released you, repeat the above steps until he does. The reverse grip with the blade pointing downward is ideal for this thrusting defensive tactic. If you are not armed, you can deliver a powerful foot stomp, breaking several bones in the criminal's foot. Thrust an elbow into his midsection. As his grip loosens, turn towards your attacker so that he is at your 9 or 3 O'clock. Now use the 9 O'clock / 3 O'clock tactic described above. If he is too close to execute the tactic, create space and distance with an elbow to any available target.

Another defensive tactic when someone grabs you from behind is to bend forward at the waist and cup your hand or interlock laced fingers around the back of the attacker's leg below his calf muscle. Now, while pulling his leg (upwards) between your legs, sit (downwards) on his leg at or just above the attacker's knee. You are pulling up with your clasped hands while squatting down. This puts a tremendous amount of stress on his knee. Pull up and sit down simultaneously until you hear or feel severe damage. This attacker approached you from behind. We do not know what his intentions were, but they were not good.

The intense pain caused may cause him to black out or fall to the ground. Let him, but do not go to the ground with him. As he collapses to the pavement, turn on the balls of your feet - placing him at your 12 O'clock. Stomp his ankle for good measure if necessary. Lastly, get out of there and call for help. Remember. This is LIFE fighting; this low life did not pick on you to spar. Unfortunately, what he wants from you, you can't get back. They wish you DEAD before you reach RED. The scum of the earth wishes for you to abide by social norms while they operate well outside of them.

Back to the clock scenarios: what if you were attacked from 8 O'clock? You launch a horizontal left elbow - connecting with his nose, or throat, or anywhere in between. Then, with a hammered fist, swiftly swing your left forearm down to his groin. You should make contact with the bottom of your fist - causing him to bend forward at the waist. Turn on the balls of your feet in order to get the crook at your 12 O'clock. Place one hand on each of his shoulders and shove him backward to the pavement. Stomp his nearest leg joint, ankle or knee before creating distance and reporting it to the police. Use this exact same defense tactic if you are attacked from your 4 O'clock. This time you will be using your right elbow and right hammer fist.

If you encounter a hostile threat at 11 or 10 O'clock, you want to take a defensive stance. The orthodox stance will be ideal. Your left leg and left fist will both be slightly forward. Establish a solid base, pushing off with your right (rear) leg, launch a rear hand punch into the nose or throat of your attacker. Now, step forward and to the left with your left leg. Grab his arms as if you were wrestling. Bring your rear leg behind the attacker and execute a swift leg sweep. Release his arms and allow him to meet the ground with great force. This exact concept works if a bad guy comes from 2 to 1 O'clock as well. As they approach from the right, allow your left fist to be your rear hand, strike (rear left hand) and then take a wide, forward left step past the opposition. Execute a powerful leg sweep. Allow the ground to do the damage. Be aware, if the Billy Bad Butt that you just took down failed to break his fall, this tactic could prove to be fatal. Understand that fully and consider this before use.

Train the entire clock defensive tactic scenario(s). If you find that you struggle with the "4 O'clock defense," work on it mentally and physically. Make modifications if necessary. There is always more than one way to take down a thug. Be careful, the more you learn the more options you have. For most people, the more choices they have, the longer it takes for them to act or make a decision. Keep it simple yet effective.

# TOPIC 6
## PREPARATION

# FIT TO FIGHT

One of my occupational specialties in the Marines was 1371 Combat Engineer. With this MOS we learned about the physiological effects of landmines. Specifically, how anti-personnel mines were designed to maim and not kill. If one member of a route clearance team was struck, two or three additional Marines would have to render aid and for the time being, no longer act in the capacity of "aggressive combatant."

This is relevant because oftentimes, bad guys work in teams of two or three. Rats travel in Packs.

If you find yourself outnumbered, be a landmine. Be an anti-personnel landmine. Take out the knee of the closest assailant so that the others have to stop their planned assault and render aid. An elevated stomping push kick will hyper-extend the thug's knee. You want him screaming and writhing in pain so that the other members stop their pursuit and assist their fellow hoodlum.

You must be prepared both mentally and physically for sudden violence. The mental part is not very difficult. Know where you are and know what "could" happen at all times. Use the Cooper Color Code. Never be in the white while you are away from home and amongst people you don't know. Even if you are in Church, you shouldn't be in the white. You don't know everyone's state of mind. The doors are not locked, they are usually opened to the public. Have a plan, go over it mentally in your head.

In order to be physically prepared, you want both strength and endurance. Kettlebell workouts promote strength and endurance simultaneously. Kettlebell workouts also enhance coordination. Hand-eye coordination is very valuable for self-defense. For the defensive tactics discussed in this book, develop upper and lower body power. This can be done without weights or a gym membership. Bodyweight squats and push-ups work wonders. When performing bodyweight squats, elevate the heels of your feet by placing each foot on a folded towel or on your shoes. This will improve your form and range of motion. Do not allow your knees to extend past your toes. Execute 90 degree bends, your thighs should be parallel to the floor as you bend. Please see the photo on the following page.

If you are not strong enough to do push-ups yet try using your wall or countertop. Please see modification examples below. **Make sure that you check with a healthcare professional before starting an exercise regimen.**

With push-ups and bodyweight squats, you would like to do 4 sets each and 10 reps per set. Take a break after each set

that is approximately half as long as it took you to do the set. For example, if you take 40 seconds to do 10 squats, rest for only 20 seconds.

Once the squats and push-ups are no longer challenging, add a weighted vest or backpack. If you were to add a 1 gallon Ziplock bag full of water, that is a little over 8lbs. per bag. Re-enforce the bag with plenty of duct tape to prevent leaks. For weighted squats, use dumbbells or wear the backpack in the front. I just hold a couple dumbbells like suitcases. Please see the photo on the following page.

The bodyweight squats directly impact your ability to execute an effective thrusting kick to an assailant's knee.

Push-ups increase the effectiveness and power of your webbed palm strike as well as your ability to push away an assailant. This could create time and space, allowing you to retrieve your weapon or think of your next move.

# TOPIC 7
## FINAL THOUGHTS AND GOOD ADVICE

## THE FOLLOWING INFORMATION IS GOOD ADVICE AND IDEAS TO CONSIDER:

- There have been incidents where law enforcement has barged into the wrong home and fired upon the occupants in error. If you hear a loud knock at your door in the middle of the night, immediately call 911. Give your address and determine if law enforcement is at your residence.

- Try to convey to dispatch that they (law enforcement) are at the wrong door.

- Establish the mindset that you are more afraid of being abducted than a physical altercation. Do not comply. Do not go with a would-be captor. Fight for your life. Sleep with your car keys near your nightstand. Press the panic button if you do not have an alarm system and you hear an intruder enter your home. Most importantly, remain mentally and physically prepared for whatever you pray never happens.

www.ingramcontent.com/pod-product-compliance
Lightning Source LLC
LaVergne TN
LVHW051040070526
838201LV00066B/4871